THE

FAMILY DYER

Reprinted 1998
Harrisonburg-Rockingham Historical Society
P.O. Box 716
Dayton, VA 22821-0716

The original copy was purchased January 9, 1998
at the estate auction of Houston S. Bowman
from Timberville, Virginia

Printed in the United States of America.

Thanks to Nancy Taylor Sorrells, Research Historian at the Museum of American Frontier Culture in Staunton, Virginia, for her assistance in reproducing this booklet, to Betty A. Garnett, HRHS volunteer, for her endless typing of the text, and to Cheryl Lyon, of LDA Creations, for her assistance in the cover design of the book.

Library of Congress Catalog Card Number: 98-71048
ISBN 0-9664149-1-8

Harrisonburg-Rockingham Historical Society
P.O. Box 716
Dayton, Virginia 22821
(540) 879-2616

First Reprinting - 1998

INTRODUCTION

At first glance the little yellowed booklet, printed in 1848, doesn't appear to be much. It measures only 5½ inches by 8 inches. The 41 pages, which are hand-stitched together, are filled with nothing more than recipes--not for food dishes, but for different colors and types of dye. But in reality, *The Family Dyer (Being a complete guide for colouring every variety of shade, on woolen, cotton, linen, and silk goods together with an appendage containing directions for discharging colours, bleaching, &c)* is a jewel. Not only does it represent an early generation of "household help" books for the Shenandoah Valley, but it is significant because of who printed it and where it was printed.

Joseph Funk (1778-1862) was a German Mennonite born in Pennsylvania. At an early age he moved to the Valley and settled in a strong German community located in Rockingham County, VA. Among his many skills, Funk was a musician and teacher of music. Today the village where he lived is called Singer's Glen in honor of the Funk family, but when Funk settled in the area it was known as Mountain Valley. The name was changed in 1860.

Fairly late in his life, starting in the 1830s, Funk launched a secondary career in the book world. In 1832 he compiled a book of church music, while in 1837 he was asked to translate some religious literature from German into English, which he did. Although he had compiled a book of church music in German in 1816, no other records of his works appear until the 1832 work. These works and others spun off into a printing, bookbinding and publishing business which he established in Mountain Valley with his sons in 1847.

No doubt many families in 19th century America entered the printing business, but Joseph Funk & Sons was unique. The business represented only the second Mennonite printing house in North America (the other one was in Ontario) and the only one printing in English. Joseph Funk was obviously astute enough to realize that the period during the 1830s and 1840s was a transitional time for many traditional German communities. Although German was still the language spoken in the homes and churches, English was the law of the land. Many of the younger generation were moving away from any use of German and adapting the language and ways of the larger American community. Funk was fluent in both languages, but his press printed nothing but English books, and with the exception of the early 1816 work, none of his compilations were in German. Clearly Funk recognized the language of the future.

As can be expected, the majority of the known works which came from Funk's presses were either religious or musical or both in nature. He began the printing business as a way to have a career for his son Joseph. After Joseph completed an apprenticeship in nearby Harrisonburg, the Funks converted a loom house into a print shop and went into business in October 1847. Their first job was printing the fourth edition of Funk's *A Compilation of Genuine Church Music* (renamed *Harmonia Sacra* in 1851). The book, which is now in its 24th edition, is probably Funk's best-known and most important contribution. The influence of *Harmonia Sacra* on the spiritual music of the South is recognized by all music historians.

The Funks soon realized that they needed to print more than their own work to make money and so they solicited other authors. They were immediately successful in this venture as well. The second book to roll off the presses, in 1848, was *The Family Dyer*. True to his earlier publications, Funk had the piece printed in English despite the fact that other books on dying, printed in German, had been successful in German-speaking areas like Pennsylvania. *The Family Dyer* enjoyed enough success that it was reprinted at least twice.

Of the fifty or so books printed on the loom-house press during Funk's lifetime, almost all were music, religious or moral in nature. Although Funk was a staunch Mennonite, he was not above printing the minutes of the Lutheran Synod or those of the Sons of Temperance. When he strayed away from those themes it was with household helpers like *The Family Dyer*. Only two other similar books appear to have been printed by the Funks. In 1852 a 48-page cookbook called *A Valuable Receipt Book, for Economical Families* was printed, and in 1853 *The Farmer's Nonpareil Packet Companion* was published. These booklets represent the practical side of the Funk business and indicate an awareness that booklets such as these, which would help make people's lives easier, would sell. Just as significantly, they are the only known booklets of this type printed in the Upper Shenandoah Valley before the Civil War.

And so, there is a lot of history stitched up in the few pages of *The Family Dyer*. Local historians value it for its meaning and place in history. Spinners, weavers and living historians will also find great value in the content. They will have fun testing and experimenting with the many hues and shades described. Either way, there's more to this little booklet than first meets the eye.

If you want to learn more about Joseph Funk and his printing press, read the following:

1. Two articles in the *EMC Bulletin*, February 1965: "Joseph Funk's Contribution to Church Music" by Harry Eskew and "Singers Glen, Virginia Imprints, 1847-1878: A Checklist," Compiled by Irvin B. Horst.
2. Horst, Irvin B., "Joseph Funk, Early Mennonite Printer and Publisher," reprint from *Mennonite Quarterly Review*, October 1957.
3. Wayland, John, *The German Element of the Shenandoah Valley*.
4. Wayland, John, *A History of Rockingham County*.

Nancy Taylor Sorrells
Research Historian
Museum of American Frontier Culture
March, 1998

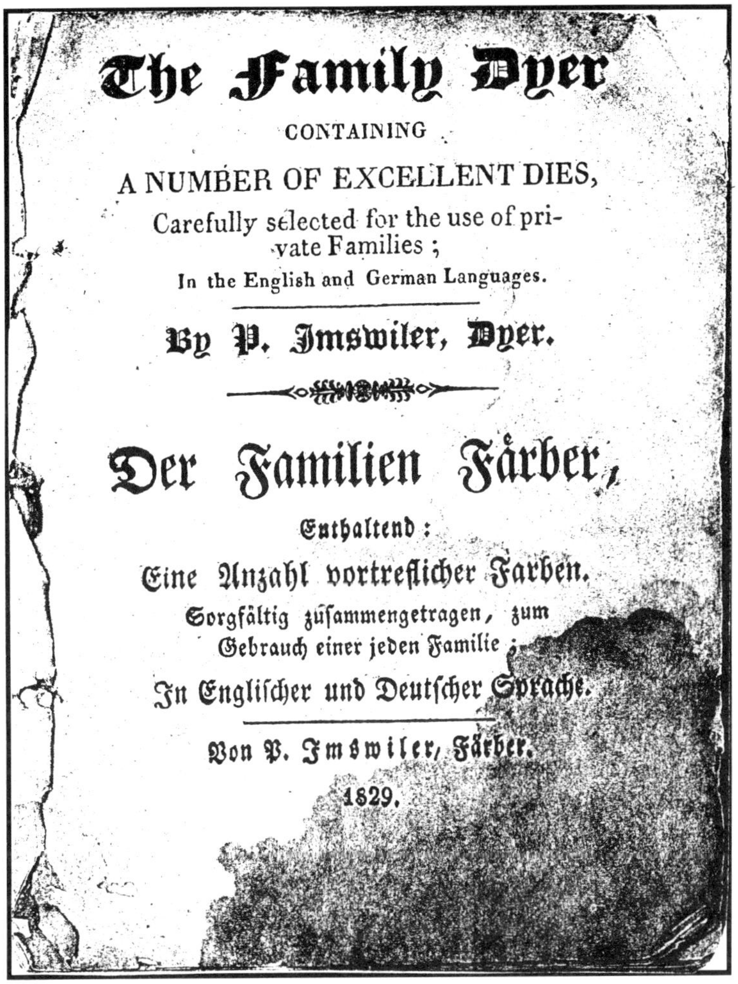
The Family Dyer

CONTAINING

A NUMBER OF EXCELLENT DIES,

Carefully selected for the use of private Families;

In the English and German Languages.

By P. Imswiler, Dyer.

Der Familien Färber,

Enthaltend:

Eine Anzahl vortreflicher Farben.

Sorgfältig zusammengetragen, zum Gebrauch einer jeden Familie;

In Englischer und Deutscher Sprache.

Von P. Imswiler, Färber.

1829.

As this 1829 book called *The Family Dyer* indicates, Joseph Funk was not the first publisher to print a book on dyeing. Although the title of this book is the same, however, the content of Funk's book is different and does not appear to be a pirated copy of this earlier German-English booklet. The 1829 book, shown here actual size, is in the collection of Eastern Mennonite University's Menno Simons Historical Library and Archives. (Printed in Pennsylvania)

The Joseph Funk printing shop was located in the community of Singers Glen (originally called Mountain Valley). Funk's shop was originally a loom house, while the ground floor served as a springhouse. Funk printed thousands of hymnals as well as other books such as *The Family Dyer* from the confines of this small printing shop.

THE

FAMILY DYER,

BEING

A COMPLETE GUIDE

FOR COLOURING EVERY VARIETY OF SHADE,

ON WOOLEN, COTTON, LINEN, AND SILK GOODS.

TOGETHER WITH

AN APPENDAGE

CONTAINING DIRECTIONS FOR DISCHARGING COLOURS,
BLEACHING, &c.

BY AN EMINENT EUROPEAN DYER.

MOUNTAIN VALLEY, NEAR HARRISONBURG, VA.

PUBLISHED BY JOSEPH FUNK & SONS.

—1848.—

The title page of *The Family Dyer* edition used for this reprint booklet is shown here actual size. The book is in the collection of the Harrisonburg-Rockingham Historical Society.

THE

FAMILY DYER,

BEING

A COMPLETE GUIDE

FOR COLOURING EVERY VARIETY OF SHADE,

ON WOOLEN, COTTON, LINEN, AND SILK GOODS.

TOGETHER WITH

AN APPENDAGE,

CONTAINING DIRECTIONS FOR DISCHARGING COLOURS.
BLEACHING, &c.

BY AN EMINENT EUROPEAN DYER.

THIRD EDITION.

MOUNTAIN VALLEY, NEAR HARRISONBURG, VA.

PUBLISHED BY JOSEPH FUNK & SONS.

—1849.—

The Family Dyer proved to be a popular enough seller that it went through three editions. The title page from the third edition is shown here actual size. The book is in the collection of Eastern Mennonite University's Menno Simons Historical Library and Archives.

THE

FAMILY DYER,

BEING

A COMPLETE GUIDE

FOR COLOURING EVERY VARIETY OF SHADE,

ON WOOLEN, COTTON, LINEN, AND SILK GOODS.

TOGETHER WITH

AN APPENDAGE

CONTAINING DIRECTIONS FOR DISCHARGING COLOURS,
BLEACHING, &c.

BY AN EMINENT EUROPEAN DYER.

MOUNTAIN VALLEY, NEAR HARRISONBURG, VA.

PUBLISHED BY JOSEPH FUNK & SONS.

--1848.--

PREFACE.

The author of the following receipts, having been a practical dyer for many years in Europe as well as in this country for twenty-two years, has had every opportunity of making improvements in the art of dyeing, and of bringing it out in its greatest perfection. And having frequently been applied to for receipts, by a great number of those who were acquainted with his perfection in the art, he concluded to give to his friends and the public, in pamplet form, a complete guide for colouring every variety of shade.

Those receipts, therefore, will instruct any one in the art of Dyeing---mixing colours---shading them, and imparting to the goods the richest hue---regularity of shade, and brilliancy of colour.

The publishers having been solicited to reprint these receipts, by those who have had the use of them for some time, they have concluded to do so, with the belief that they will prove to be a benefit to all those into whose hands they may come; and thus be instrumental in promoting home industry and domestic manufacture. It must bc a source of great gratification to every housewife to be ablc to furnish her house with all necessary articles of her own manufacture, which can vie, in richness and durability of colour, with the most brilliant of European manufacture.

RECOMMENDATIONS.

We the undersigned having practiced, for a number of years, the different receipts for colouring on the following pages, do hereby testify that we have found them to answer the description admirably well. The colours are rich, brilliant, and durable, and will compete with foreign colouring, either on woolen, cotton, linen, or silk. We can therefore recommend them to the public with the belief that they will prove to be a great acquisition to domestic manufacturing.

SUSAN BOWMAN.
ELIZABETH A. HOPKINS.
HESTER BOWMAN.
HANNAH J. BEAR.
NANCY CRAWFORD.

Rockingham County,
Virginia, 1848.

EXPLANATION OF CHEMICAL NAMES---
MORDANTS.

Those that want no mordant or preparation are, black, slate, drab, ash, and buff colours. There are some red and yellow dyes without a mordant, for which a Chemical (sic) process is made by way of a solution of tin, which fixes the colour quick, and makes it a glossy and shining colour; but the alkali will always be injurious to the brilliancy of the colour; but before giving any receipts, I will give an explanation of the Chemical names, as in my receipts I shall mostly give the Chemical names, and not only for that reason, but all the modern receipts of any kind are mostly given in Chemical names, which will make every one acquainted with them.

CHEMICAL NAMES.	EXPLANATION OR COMMON NAMES.
Nitrate of Iron, . .	Iron dissolved in Nitric Acid.
Acetate of Alumine, .	{A mixture of one part Sugar of Lead and { two parts of Alum.
Sulphate of Lime, . .	Lime saturated with Sulphuric Acid.
Oxide of Iron, . .	{Any thing that has a strong tendency of Iron { such as iron dissolved in Vinegar, { Copperas, &c.
Sulphuret of Arsenic, .	Orpiment.
Spirit of Hartshorn, .	Spirit of Sal ammoniac, an animal Alkali.
Nitric Acid, . . .	Aqua-Fortis.
Sulphuric Acid, . .	Oil of Vitriol.
Muriatic Acid, . .	Spirit of Salts.
Murio Sulphate Tin, .	{Two parts Sulphuric Acid, three parts Muriatic, { and Tin as much as it will dissolve.
Nitro Muriate of Tin, .	{Two parts Aqua-fortis, one part Sp't Salt, { & one-eighth of its weight of Tin.
Muriate of Tin, . .	One lb. Sp't Salt---two oz. Tin dissolved in it.
Sulphate of Zinc, . .	White Vitriol.
Sulphate of Indigo, .	{Indigo fermented with Oil of Vitriol called { Chemic.
Sulphate of Iron, . .	{Iron dissolved with Oil of Vitriol then { crystallized, (Copperas.)
Sulphate of Copper, .	{Copper dissolved with Oil of Vitriol, then { Crystallized, (Blue Vitriol)
Sulphate of Alumine, .	{The raw Alum decomposed with Oil of Vitriol { --common Alum.
Acetate of Iron, . .	Iron dissolved in Vinegar, (Iron Liquor.)
Acetate of Lead, . .	Lead dissolved in Vinegar, (Sugar of Lead.)
Argol, ...	Crude Tartar.
Acetate of Copper, . .	Copper dissolved in Vinegar, (Verdigris.)
Quercitron Bark, . .	Black-oak Bark.
Sulphur, . . .	Brimstone.
Fustick, . . .	Yellow dye-wood.

DYESTUFFS, SOLUTIONS, &C.

GLUE.

Animal Glue, . .	Common Glue.
Isinglass, . . .	Fish Glue.
	{Gum Arabic, from a tree in Arabia.
Vegetable Glue, . .	{Gum Dragon, from a tree in Brazil.
	{Gum Senegal, from a tree in Brazil.

DYE STUFFS.

Madder, a root---crop madder the best. It discharges three colours; hand warm a dull yellow; boiling heat its right colour, red; and boiling a red-brown. It must have a mordant to receive the colour. With yellow it makes an orange.---Tumeric, a yellow root, makes a scarlet with Cochineal; it makes a dye by itself with alum, but a fugitive yellow.---Cochineal, an insect used for dyeing scarlet, crimson, pink, rose, purple, and peach-blossom. Sac dyes make a more permanent scarlet than cochineal.

Brazil, Braziletto, Nicaragua, Cam-wood, Bear-wood, Sanders, and Peach-wood, are all more or less for red or brown, with or with-out a mordant. Logwood, Sumac, Elder, Alder, Walnut hulls, Oak bark, &c., are used for browns, drabs, and blacks. Aranetta is employed to give the first tint to woolen stuffs, intended to be dyed red, blue, yellow, and green.

SOLUTION OF TIN.

I will now give the different solutions of Tin, which will be distinguished by No. 1, 2, 3.

No. 1.---Nitro Muriate of Tin.---Take 1 lb. nitric acid to 1-2 lb. muriatic acid, mix these two ingredients together in a pitcher, then add by degrees 4 oz. granulated tin---put therein a piece as big as a bean, when that is dissolved add more, till all is dissolved, then put it in a bottle well corked---it is then ready for use.

No. 2.---Murio Sulphate of Tin.---Take 3 lb. muriatic acid, to 2 lb. sulphuric acid, put the muriatic acid into a bottle sufficiently large so that it gets only half full; then put the bottle in cold water as deep as the spirit rises on the inside, then add to it the sulphuric acid---when mixed take out the bottle and put it into a warm place, or in warm water, then add granulated tin, and as it dissolves add more until it will dissolve no more. Then put the clear solution in another bottle, and it is ready for use.

The tin which is left in the sediment can be used again for another solution, if the bottle is not put in cold water. When the sulphuric acid is mixed with the muriatic, it will make a great effervescence, and is likely to burst the bottle, likewise if too much tin be put in at once it is liable to the same accident.

SOLUTIONS AND VATS.

No. 3.---Muriate of Tin.---Take 8 oz. muriatic acid, mix with it 1 oz. of water, dissolve therein 1 oz. granulated tin, little at a time until all is dissolved, when it is ready for use. Stop the bottles well with stoppers made of bees-wax (sic) and tallow melted together.

The tin for this purpose is called block tin and can generally be procured of Copper-smiths or Apothecaries. It is melted in an iron ladle, or any iron vessel, and when melted, it is held four or five feet above a tin bucket full of cold water into which the tin is then poured in a stream as thick as a straw, then pour off the water and dry the fine grain tin, after which it is ready for use. The above solutions of tin I have found to be the best that have ever been published. I used them for twenty-two years in this country. They are partly taken from Dr. Bancroft, an eminent Chemist from England who travelled in this country some years since, in search of dye-stuffs.

Besides the above solutions, there is another necessary for dyeing Saxon blue and different shades of green, and is commonly called Chemic, because it was first discovered by a chemist in the Kingdom of Saxony, but the right name is Sulphate of Indigo, because the indigo is decomposed and fermented by sulphuric acid, which solution I shall now likewise describe.

No. 4.---Sulphate of Indigo, or Chemic.---Take 1 oz. Spanish Flotant indigo, which is the softest, and therefore the best, with 4 oz. sulphuric acid. Pound the indigo as fine as flour and put it in a bowl, then add the sulphuric acid by degrees to the indigo and stir it constantly with a willow rod off of which the bark has cleanly been taken, until it is well mixed, then put it in a warm place for 12 hours after which add one gill of cold water, but very slowly, and as the solution rises stir it constantly until it settles again, then put it in a bottle for use.

Having given a sufficient description as an introduction to the art of dyeing, I will now pass to the more useful description and the receipts, and shall commence with the two primitive colours, with their different shades, and afterwards the compound colours, such as brown, green purple, &c.

No. 5.---Blue, Warm or Ash Vat.---Take 1 lb. of indigo, best Bengal, pound it fine, then put it in an iron pot, put 1-2 pints boiling water thereon, let it soak for half an hour, then run a round ball in the pot, or rub it with some other round instrument. When it becomes considerably fine put about one gallon of water thereon, wash the ball or instrument used in the pot likewise, then beat it with a stick which will give the pot a trembling motion, and will settle the indigo, which is not yet fine enough, decant off the blue liquid into your vat; then grind the thick parts again, and so on until you can feel no grit any more between your fingers, put them all in your vat, wash all the indigo into it, then take a boiler that will hold about 12 or 15 gallons, fill it nearly full of water, then add to it 1 lb of madder, 8 handfuls of wheat bran, and 3-4 lb. potash; boil this together for five minutes but so that it does not boil over, then put it to your indigo in your vat---rick it up and cover it well, and keep the vat constantly in a heat that you can just bear your hand in it. In two hours rick it up again, and so on for three or four times. By this time the blue vat will have a copperas rind, and by raising the liquid towards the light it will look green.

When a blue vat has this appearance, fill your boiler again with water and put therein 1 1-4 lb. potash. After this is dissolved put two quarts of it into your vat, then rick it up well and let it stand for two hours---put in again two or three quarts---rick again, and keep on in this manner until all your liquor is in the vat, (the potash liquor must always be hot), then the vat will look yellow; by raising the liquid to the light it will have a very handsome copper skin and purple fume on top, and a strong fermenting smell; then take out your ricker, and in two hours more the vat is ready to dip. Care must then be taken in dipping that the goods do not disturb the sediment, and as soon as the liquor gets cloudy in the vat, you must quit dipping, rick it up well, and as soon as clear again, which will be in one or two hours, you can dip again. When your vat is half spent you must add a little more potash. It will take about 2 lb. of potash to 1 lb. of indigo, or 3 lb. of pearlash, or 5 gallons of wood lie strong enough to bear an egg. In all cases you must take about the half to the boiling---first with madder and bran, which is called setting the vat, and the last kettle full is to sharpen it up. When it is sharp enough it must have these signs, it must feel a little slippery between your fingers and bite a little on your tongue.

RENEW A VAT

If there is not indigo enough in the vat to finish your goods and you should wish to finish them, you can take 1-4 or 1-2 lb. of indigo more, after it is made fine put it in the vat, and for 1-2 lb. indigo take 1-2 lb madder, 4 handfuls wheat bran, 2 quarts lie, 4 gallons water, boil it together for five minutes, then put it in the vat, rick it up and sharpen it as before until sharp enough. Should it happen that the vat does not work at first, then you have either too much or too little lie in it---some indigo takes more alkali, and some less---if you have too much lie in it, and it does not work in six hours it will feel very slippery between your fingers and smell very strong, then you take two quarts of bran, put boiling water over it, stir it up and put it in the vat, rick it up, and in two hours it will surely work. In case it is not sharp enough in the beginning, the vat will look thin and have a sour smell, then you must add more lie, and begin to sharpen sooner, as above directed. If a dye should be over charged, that it has too much lie in it, so that the liquid looks black and bran will have no effect upon it, then you must take out the clear liquid into a vessel, then put the sediment into another vessel, put the clear liquid back into the vat again---boil off 1-4 lb. madder, 4 handfuls of wheat bran, 1 pint of lie, in 4 gallons of water, put it in the vat, and then there is nothing to hinder it from working; then sharpen as before. After you colour, put one quart of that sediment which you took out before, back again into the vat every other dip, until all is in again, so that you will lose none of the indigo. If you will set a blue vat again, take three or four buckets full of your old clear dye out, and after you empty the vat, put that clear dye back again. It will make your vat quicker and surer, by observing the foregoing well. Grind the indigo fine, and keep all the vessels clean, and keep your vat in an equal heat. There is no danger of losing a blue vat---I never lost one in my life.

The above ash vat will colour wool, linen, cotton and silk. The cotton goods must be boiled first, the woolen well washed and scoured, and the silk run first through hot water. They must be entered wet, but previously well wrung and dipped until dark enough.

VATS---COLD DYE.

No. 6.---Blue Indigo Vat---Cold Dye.---I shall give a blue vat here, which colours nothing but cotton, linen and silk---is used cold, and is in no ways so difficult as the warm ash vat. The light blue is dyed handsomer and more brilliant than in the ash vat, and likewise the pale blue is dyed in this vat for a good standing green on silk, cotton, and linen. Another advantage in this vat is, that you can colour out of it when you please, once a week, or once a month, and is handy for any housewife. In this vat all blue calicoes are dyed and all blue domestic checks.

I shall give the receipt for one pound of indigo, which can be set in a barrel that holds about thirty gallons. A cider of (sic) whiskey barrel is as good as any and easily procured. One head must be taken out of the barrel, and the bung hole well secured. The barrel should be well bound and set on blocks in a cellar or some damp place.

Take 1 lb. of indigo, Bengal is always the best, grind it fine, as described in No. 5, put the blue indigo liquid in the barrel, then fill the barrel up with fresh water within about twelve inches, then dissolve 3 lb. of copperas in 1 gallon of hot water, put it into your vat to the indigo liquor, rick it up with a small rake, then take 3 lb. of unslacked lime, slack it in another gallon of water, and put it likewise into the vat---rick it again, and so keep on every two hours for ten hours, then take out the rick, and in six hours it will be settled enough for colouring. The vat will then have a copper skin, and a purple scum on top, and by raising the liquid it will look yellow. Have your cotton well boiled and wrung, hand it on sticks in the dye and let them rest on the top of the barrel; turn your cotton, linen, or silk until the liquid is exhausted, then ring your yarn out well into the dye and rick it up well. If your yarn is not dark enough, wrap it into a cloth, and in six hours you can dip it again. When it is sufficiently dark wash it in clean water, then wring it well and dry it. Your barrel should be within three inches full, and when not colouring, should be covered with a board. You can let it stand for months, and on the evening before you wish to colour, rick up the dye as abovementioned, and when exhausted, dissolve 3-4 lb. copperas and 3-4 lb. lime into it. You can afterwards put into the same liquid another 1 2 lb. of indigo with 1 1-2 lb. of copperas, and 1 1-2 lb. unslacked lime, in the same manner as above described.---There is a great difference in indigo, some is very hard, and heavy to its bulk, which is commonly mixed with slate, and is of a blackish colour, which sort is in no wise good for colouring; some is of a dark blue purple, in square lumpts, light to its bulk, easily broken, a little whitish in streaks inside, which is the best, called Bengal.

No. 7.---Chamber Lye---Blue Vat.---As I have now given a description of two of the best blue vats, I will give another which the economical housewife very often uses, and is only used for woolen. For this purpose have an iron vessel filled with chamber-lie, put it in a warm place, in summer heat in the sun, and in cold weather in a corner in the fireplace. After standing three or four days, take off the clear lie and throw away the sediment, then have your indigo finely pounded, put it in a fine linen or cotton bag and lay it in the lie. If you have 1-4 lb. of indigo, put in another bag 1-4 of madder and 2 handfuls of wheat bran, put it in the lie, size both of your bags every day two or three times. In the course of five or six days your liquor will look green, then take out the bags and put in your wool for two, three, or four hours, take out the wool, wring it hard into the dye, then put the bags in again, sizing them once or twice, and if your wool is not dark enough dip it again.

If your liquor gives out, which will be the case, fill it up with chamber-lie that has been previously settled. By settling the lie first it will take away the disagreeable animal smell. Wash your wool afterwards in soap suds, and then rinse it in clear water.

I come now to those colours which require boiling, some with, and some without a mordant, and I shall generally give receipts for 5 lb. of woolen yarn, which will be equal to six lb. of woolen cloth. If goods are wove into a cotton or linen chain or warp, the chain must be deducted, as the cotton or linen does not receive the colour in a woolen dye.

No. 8.---Saxon or Chemic Blue.---Fill your copper boiler which holds a sufficiency of water to float your goods with water, dissolve therein 1 lb. of alum, after dissolved, put in your goods and boil for two hours, then take out and rinse them, then fill your boiler with fresh water and put therein as much of the above described sulphate of indigo or Chemic, (No. 4,) as you wish the shade for your colour; when it is hand hot, enter your goods and boil them for half an hour, then take them out and scrape a piece of chalk about as big as a hickory nut, then enter your goods again and boil five minutes longer---air, drain, and wash them clean.

Remark---When you first put in your Chemic, stir it up and you will see in the liquid exactly the colour it will make; keep it always a shade lighter than the colour required. If not dark enough---you will perceive it in five minutes' boiling---take out your goods and add more Chemic, in that way you can make any shade from the lightest to the darkest blue. It is only a pity that this colour will not stand washing in alkali.

No. 9.---Navy Blue.---To 5 lb. of woolen yarn take 3-4 lb. of alum, 3 oz. crude tartar in your boiler filled with water, boil your goods therein for one hour, take them out and rinse them, then fill your boiler with fresh water and boil therein 3 lb. of ground logwood for 30 or 40 minutes---take out the chips, raise your dye with 1-4 lb. of blue stone, or 1-4 lb. of verdigris, then enter your goods, boil them one hour, then wash them clean.

Having now given all the necessary receipts for blue on wool, I will give receipts for the other primitive colour, red.

No. 10.---Madder Red.---To 5 lb. woolen yarn, take 1 1-4 lb. of alum and 5 oz. crude tartar, dissolve them and put them in your boiler---enter your yarn and boil it for two hours, then take it out, drain it, and wrap it up in a cloth and lay it away in a damp place for three or four days, thus the mordant will impregnate the yarn. After that time you rinse your yarn well in a running stream, then fill your boiler with water, put therein 1 1-2 lb. of crop madder; as soon as milk warm put your yarn on sticks across the boiler; let the sticks rest on the top thereof, and the yarn hang in the dye---turn your yarn constantly and regulate your fire so that it will come to a boiling heat. In one hour lay your yarn in the dye for five or ten minutes, turning it with a stick, then take it out, air it and wash it clean, and you will have a very handsome red if the madder is good. This is as good a colour as the alkali blue; it will resist any chemical agent, as well as soap and air.

As it often happens that crude tartar is not to be had in the country, there is a substitute for it: three or four days previous to your colouring take one gallon of wheat bran, scald it with three gallons of hot water and let it ferment in a warm place, which soon turns it sour, add then to the alum, instead of the crude tartar, one quart to every pound of yarn and proceed as above.

No. 11.---Madder Red-Brown.---A handsome and permanent brown is made for linsey, by taking 4 oz. of logwood---boil it fifteen minutes, remove the chips, then add to this logwood decoction 4 oz. of copperas; after your madder red (No. 10) is coloured, put of this logwood and copperas liquor in the madder dye and boil it for ten minutes. Your colour will be darker in proportion to the quantity of this liquor which you put into the dye.

No. 12.---Scarlet, with Sac-Dye.---To 1 lb. of yarn for this colour (your boiler must be well secured, and very clean; then fill it with clean water,) take 2 1-2 oz. Sac-dye into a bowl or pitcher, put hot water thereon, stir it well and mix it with the water---it is hard to mix owing to the gummy substance which attends the lac---when well mixed and the water in your boiler is hand hot, put it in the boiler and add thereto 2 oz. cream of tartar, boil it for five minutes, then add 1 qt. strong decoction of black-oak bark and 3 oz. of the solution Muria Sulphate of tin, (No. 2,) then enter your previously wetted yarn and boil it about 1 1-2 or 2 hours, then wash it clean. This scarlet will stand washing in soap, is very handsome, and will not turn crimson like the following cochineal scarlet with alkali, and is considerably cheaper.

No. 13.---Scarlet, With Cochineal.---To 1 lb. of yarn---have your boiler very clean and filled with water---when hot put therein 1 oz. of cochineal previously made fine in a coffee-mill or a mortar, boil it for a few minutes and then add 2 oz. cream of tartar and 3-4 oz. of tumeric, stir it and add 3 oz. of Nitro Muriate of tin---solution of tin, No. 1.---Boil your previously wetted yarn half an hour therein; wash it clean. By putting in this exhausted liquor 2 oz. of alum and 1-4 oz. of pearlash, you can make a pretty pink by boiling yarn therein for 15 minutes.

No. 14.---Wood Red.---To 5 lb.---Take 1 1-4 lb. of alum, 5 qt. of sour water, as in remark No. 10, boil your yarn for two hours, then wrap it up and put it in a cool place for three or four days, then rinse it. Boil off 3 lb. of Brazil wood for two hours, then take out the chips and add to the dye 2 oz. of alum, after dissolved boil your yarn therein for two hours, then wash it clean. Remark.---By adding 1-2 lb. of madder to the Brazil liquor after the chips are taken out, it will make the colour more permanent.

No. 15.---Light Red.---Yarn that is previously prepared with alum and cream of tartar or sour water, as in No. 14, and boiled in this exhausted liquor for one hour, will make a fine light red, a handsome lighter shade for carpeting.

COLOURING RECEIPTS.

No. 16.---Blood Red.---To 5 lb.---Boil your yarn for 2 hours in 1 1-4 lb. of alum and 5 qt. of sour water, or 4 oz. crude tartar, rinse it, after which, take 4 oz. of aranetta, rub it between your hands in warm water until dissolved, put it in the boiler, and add 2 oz. pot-ash, or 4 oz. pearl-ash, or 2 qt. strong lie, stir it up and boil your yarn for half an hour; then make a fresh liquor with 4 lb. Brazil wood; boil the wood in water for two hours, and after taking out the chips, boil your yarn therein for two hours, which makes a very pretty colour.

No. 17.---Crimson.---Crimson is dyed red either by No. 10, 14, 15, or 16; then fill your boiler with water and when boiling hot put therein, for 5 lb. of yarn, 1-2 lb. of hard soap previously dissolved in chamber lye, run your yarn in it for ten minutes, then wash it clean. This is a colour very much used for linsey filled on a blue cotton chain.

No. 18.---Crimson, with Cochineal.---To 5 lb. fine goods.---Have your boiler clean and filled with water, dissolve therein 6 oz. of alum, 4 oz. cream of tartar, 1 1-2 oz. cochineal finely powdered; boil these up together, then add 6 oz. solution of tin, No. 1, enter your yarn previously wetted, and boil it for one hour, then boil 1 lb. of Brazil wood, for two hours; after removing the chips, add 2 oz. of alum and 4 oz. of pearlash, then enter your yarn and boil it for an hour, and wash it clean.

No. 19.---Another.---To 5 lb.---A full crimson is made of cochineal for fine goods: fill your boiler with water, dissolve therein 1 lb. alum 6 oz. solution of tin, No. 1, boil your yarn therein for one hour, then put fresh water in your boiler and put therein 5 oz. of fine powdered cochineal, boil it, and add 4 oz. of alum, and 3 oz. solution of tin, No. 1, boil it for one hour more, then wash it clean. If you want it more bluish add 2 oz. of pearlash.

No. 20.---Pink.---By adding to the dye, No. 19, 4 oz. more of alum, and 2 oz. of pearlash, you can have a beautiful pink by boiling white yarn therein.

No. 21.---Another Pink.---To 5 lb.---Take 10 oz. of alum, 5 oz. cream of tartar, 2 1-2 oz. of ground cochineal, boil them five minutes; then add 2 oz. solution of tin, No. 1, boil your wet yarn therein for one hour, you will have a fine colour, then wash it clean.

After No. 21 is coloured, put in the same liquor 5 oz. of alum, 2 1-2 oz. cream of tartar, after dissolved it will colour 3 lb. more of a lighter shade, by boiling it half an hour therein.

Note.---by adding to this dye a little alkali, potash, pearlash, or lime water, it will always make different shades, so that you can variegate your shades at pleasure.

No. 22.---Rose Colour.---To 5 lb.---After your kettle is cleaned fill it with water, when boiling hot put therein 2 1-2 oz. of powdered cochineal, 5 oz. cream of tartar, boil it up, then add 10 oz. solution of tin, No. 1, boil your wet yarn therein for one hour, then wash it clean.

No. 23.---Wine Colour.---To 5 lb.---Colour the yarn a pink as in No. 21; then have fresh water in your boiler, add thereto 1 1-2 lb. of madder, boil your pink yarn therein for one hour, and you will have a rich wine colour.

No. 24.---Orange.---To 5 lb.---Make strong solution of black-oak bark, which liquor will look very brown. After taking out the bark, add four oz. of alum, and 10 oz. solution of tin, No. 2, stir it, then enter your wet yarn, boil it for five minutes, take it out, and wash it clean. This colour strikes very quick, and is very brilliant. The handsome yellow flannen seen in stores is of this dye.

No. 25.---Another.---This is nearly as pretty as No. 24, and is made thus: make a strong decoction of black-oak bark, then add 1 lb. of alum, after dissolved scrape therein a lump of chalk as big as a walnut, then enter your yarn and boil for ten minutes. These two colours, No. 24 and 25, will make different shades, from the natural orange to the lightest straw colour. Take out the orange after five minutes' boiling, then add 2 oz. of alum, and 5 oz. solution of tin, or instead thereof more chalk, enter 4 lb. of yarn and it will make the next shade; take this out after five minutes boiling; add to the same liquor 1 oz. of alum and 2 oz. solution of tin, which will still give a lighter shade, and will be as brilliant as the other. Care should be taken that the outside of the bark is shaved off, or it will make the colour too brown.

No. 26.---Yellow.---To 5 lb.---Boil your yarn in 1 1-4 lb. of alum and 4 oz. cream of tartar, for 2 hours, rinse it; then boil off 1 1-2 lb. Fustick in sufficient water for one hour, take out the chips, add 2 oz. of alum to raise the colour, then enter your yarn and boil for half an hour, wash it clean. This is a dull colour, but it makes a very good standing dark yellow.

No. 27.---Orange.---Take the yarn dyed in No. 26, and run it fifteen minutes through the exhausted red liquor, No. 10 or 14, where the yarn has been dyed, but the madder dye is the best.

No. 28.---Dark Orange, With Cochineal.---To 5 lb.---For fine goods make a decoction of black-oak bark, boil the bark only five minutes, take it out and add 4 oz. of alum and 2 oz. of powdered cochineal, boil them for a few minutes, then add 10 oz. solution of tin, No. 2, enter your yarn and boil it for 15 or 20 minutes, take it out and wash it clean; then add to the same liquor 2 oz. of alum 5 oz. solution of tin, No. 2, enter other wet yarn and boil it for half an hour, which will likewise make a pretty light shade.

No. 29.---Buff.---To 5 lb.---Fill your boiler, put therein 4 oz. of alum, 4 oz. of crude tartar and 8 oz. solution of tin, No. 3, boil your yarn therein for half an hour, rinse it; then fill your boiler again and boil off 8 oz. of fustick for half an hour, take out the chips, add 2 oz. of madder, then run your goods through it for eight minutes, and wash them clean.

No. 30.---Another---Boil off 10 oz. of fustick, take out the chips, add 3 oz. madder, run your goods through it for five or ten minutes, then wash them clean.

No. 31.---Buff Brown.---To 5 lb.---Make a tolerably strong solution of sumac, boil off fustick or black-oak bark, by itself, put to the sumac liquor as much as you deem proper to make the shade, then add 2, 3, or 4 oz. of madder, according to the shade required, run your goods therein for ten minutes, then take it out, darkening off with blue-stone. Remark.---This colour can be made of different shades, and they are all very handsome. You can make them redder by adding more madder or more yellow, or darker by blue-stone. By using a little copperas and logwood to darken it off, it will make another shade inclining to cinnamon.

Fullers should dye this colour, which ought to be made darker for linsey or cloth.

No. 32.---Best Purple.---To 5 lb. of fine goods.---Dye your goods in the warm blue vat, No. 5, a light middle blue, wash it well in warm water, as cloth in the fulling stock, then prepare your boiler with water, when boiling put in 4 oz. of cochineal finely ground, 4 oz. of alum, 4 oz. cream of tartar, 15 oz. solution of tin, No. 1, then enter your goods and boil them for half an hour. This makes a beautiful colour, and is only used for fine broad-cloths; it should be dyed blue first, then fulled and dyed in the scarlet dye, as before described.

No. 33.---Common purple.---To 5 lb.---Prepare your goods, with 1 lb. of alum, 4 oz. of crude tartar, then boil them therein for two hours, rinse them. Then fill your boiler and boil off 8 oz. of Brazil wood, take out the chips, and add 2 oz. of ground cochineal, 8 oz. solution of tin, No. 1, boil these together, then enter your goods and boil for one hour; then empty your boiler and fill it with fresh water, boil off therein 1 lb. of logwood for half an hour, take out the chips, raise the colour with 2 oz. of alum, then add 5 oz. of chemic, let it boil up, and then enter your red goods, and run them for one hour. By this time it will be a handsome colour; finish by washing.

No. 34.---Another.---This colour I prefer for common goods, as it is sufficiently permanent. Dye your goods in a warm blue vat, No. 5 or 7, a pale blue, wash them clean, then take 1 1-2 lb. of alum 5 oz. of crude tartar, dissolve them in a sufficient quantity of water, boil your goods therein for 2 hours, rinse them well. Then fill your boiler and boil off 2 1-2 lb. of Brazil wood for two hours, take out the chips and boil your goods for one hour therein---you can improve the colour by adding 1-2 lb. madder to the Brazil liquor---then boil off 2 lb. of logwood, raise the colour with 2 oz. of alum, boil your goods for one hour, which will make a very handsome colour, especially for linsey.

No. 35.---Common purple.---To 5 lb.---Prepare your yarn in 1 lb. of alum, and 5 oz. of crude tartar by boiling it for two hours, rinse it; then boil off 2 lb. of logwood for three quarters of an hour, take out the chips, and raise the colour with 2 oz. of alum, then enter your yarn and boil it for one hour, then wash it clean.

No. 36.---Lilack.---To 5 lb.---Lilack is a lighter shade of purple and the best in fine goods, and is made in this manner: dye your goods a pale blue in the blue vat, No. 5 or 7, wash them well; then fill your boiler with water. When boiling put therein 2 1-2 oz. of ground cochineal, 6 oz. cream of tartar, 8 oz. solution to tin, No. 2, then enter your pale yarn, boil it one hour,then wash it. You can made this of different shades by making the pale blue lighter and reducing the red.

No. 37.---Another.---Pale blue your yarn, as in No. 36, wash it, then prepare it by boiling in 1 lb. of alum, and 4 oz. of crude tartar, for 2 hours, wash it; then boil off 1 lb. of Brazil and 1 lb. of logwood, take out the chips, then raise the colour with 2 oz. of alum, boil your goods therein for one hour, then wash.

You can likewise make different shades of this lilack, by increasing or decreasing the Brazil and logwood.

No. 38.---Common Lilack.---To 5 lb.---Boil 1 lb. of logwood in sufficient water for half an hour, take out the chips and dissolve in the dye 5 oz. of alum boil your yarn therein for about an hour. A lighter shade can be made out of the same liquor.

No. 39.---Lilack from Cudbear.---To 5 lb.---Fill your boiler with water, when hot put therein 10 oz. of cudbear, add one gallon of chamber lye, boil your yarn therein for two hours, which makes a good and cheap colour. The cudbear resembles sac dye, but looks more blue, and before it is put into the boiler, it ought first to be mixed with hot water in a bowl or pitcher, on account of the gum which is united with it.

No. 40.---Peach Blossom.---This is made in the same liquor after lilack is dyed out of No. 39, and if you have to make it fresh take 1 oz. of cudber (sic) per pound, instead of two as in No. 39. Cudbear will likewise make it pretty.

No. 41.---Claret.---To 5 lb.---Take 1 1-4 lb. cudbear, mix it with hot water, then put it in the boiler and boil it for one hour, then enter your yarn and boil it for two hours, air and wash it clean.

No. 42.---Cudbear ground for indigo blue, by colouring yarn or cloth which is to be an indigo blue, as claret, with 2 oz. to the pound, the same as in No. 41, takes less indigo, and makes a more firy blue; it gives it that firy blue which is so much admired. Broadcloth in Europe is mostly grounded with cudbear.

No. 43.---Claret.---To 5 lb.---Boil off 3-4 lb. Brazil and 3-4 lb. of logwood for one hour and a half, take out the chips, add 3-4 lb. of alum, 2 1-2 oz. of crude tartar, then boil your goods therein for two hours: then boil off again for a fresh liquor 1 lb. of Brazil for two hours, take out the chips, add 3 oz. of madder and 3 oz. of pearlash, boil again for one hour, then wash.

No. 44.---Another.---Take 1 1-2 lb. bearwood, boil it for fifteen minutes, add 3 oz. cream of tartar, boil your yarn for two hours therein, darken it with 2 oz. of copperas.

No. 45.---Claret Brown.---To 5 lb.---Boil 2 lb. of bearwood for ten minutes, enter your yarn and boil it for two hours, then darken it off with 4 oz. of copperas.

No. 46.---Dark Brown.---To 5 lb.---Boil 1 1-2 lb. bearwood and 1-2 lb. of fustick for one hour, then add 4 oz. of alum, enter your goods and boil them for half an hour; take them out and have a decoction made of 4 oz. of logwood, put this to your dye, then boil your goods again for half an hour, rinse them, and add 4 oz. of copperas, and boil again fifteen minutes, then air and wash them well.

Before I go any farther with the receipts for brown I must make a remark or two to the dyer. Every dyer commonly colours after a sample. If he is a little practiced he will see directly what dyestuffs are used to produce the colour; in red-browns the red is the strongest dye; if it is mixed with yellow you will see how many shades of either dye are used. For example, in that dark brown, No. 46, there are four shades of red, and one and a half yellow; then the darkening or sadening is immaterial, which you can do more or less. If there would be more yellow, it would come to the shade of a snuff brown; more yellow and logwood, and less red, to a brown; olive, no red at all to olive. It is therefore the most convenient for dyers, especially in factories, to have the liquor for darkening always ready at hand, that by darkening the goods you can raise them out, cool them off, and darken them as much as you think proper. Use rather too little at first, as you can easily add more afterwards. For browns, bottle greens, and olives: the goods should be a shade lighter than the sample, for the press will darken it a shade. For darkening I found it best to boil off 1 lb. of logwood for half an hour, in three gallons of water, take out the chips and add 2 oz. of blue stone and 4 oz. of copperas, which you can likewise use for drabs. Old black dye, for course goods, will do to darken off the colours.

No. 47.---Corbeaus or Dark Brown.---To 5 lb.---Boil 3 1-2 lb. bearwood and 4 oz. fustick for ten minutes, enter your yarn and boil it for one hour, then raise and cool it, and add the decoction of one lb. of logwood and 4 oz. of copperas, enter your yarn again and boil it for half an hour, then wash clean.

No. 48.---Dark brown, Very Handsome.---To 5 lb.---Boil 8 oz. of cam wood, 8 oz. of saunders, 4 oz. madder, 4 oz. Brazil, 8 oz. fustick for two hours, then add 4 oz. of alum and boil your goods for one hour, then add a decoction of 1 lb. of logwood, 4 oz. of copperas, then boil it again for half an hour, air and wash it well.

No. 49.----Middle Brown.---To 5 lb.---Take 4 oz. cam wood, 4 do. saunders, and 4 do. Brazil, boil them together for one hour, then add 4 oz. of madder, raise your colour with 4 oz.

of alum, enter your goods and boil for one hour, then cool them off and darken with a decoction of 1-2 lb. of logwood and 2 oz. of copperas.

No. 50.---Light Brown.---To 5 lb.---Boil your yarn for 2 hours in a preparation of 3-4 lb. of alum, and 3 oz. of crude tartar, raise it; then boil 4 oz. of saunders, 8 do. of cam wood, 4 do. of Brazil, and 4 do. of fustick, for one hour, add 4 oz. of madder, raise the colour with 2 do. of alum, enter your goods, boil them for one hour; take them out and cool, then darken with a decoction of 1-2 lb. of logwood, and 2 oz. of copperas.

No. 51.---London Brown.---To 5 lb.---Boil for one hour 8 oz. of saunders, 4 do. of cam wood, 8 do. of Brazil, and 2 do. of fustick, then add 8 oz. of madder, raise your colour with 5 do. of alum, enter your goods and boil them for one hour; cool and darken with 1-2 lb. of logwood, 2 oz. of blue stone and 2 do. of copperas.

No. 52.---Spanish Brown.---To 5 lb.---Boil 1 lb. of saunders, 4 oz. of Brazil, and 4 do. of camwood for one hour, add 8 do. of madder; raise your colour with 5 do. of alum, then boil your goods for one hour, darken with 2 oz. of logwood and 8 do. of copperas.

Note.---After you put the darkening in your dye you must always boil for 30 or 40 minutes more and always wash the goods clean.

No. 53.---Mulberry Brown.---To 5 lb.---Boil 1 lb. of saunders, 1-2 lb. Nicaragua for one hour, then add 4 oz. of madder, 4 do. of alum, 4 do. of crude tartar, boil your goods for one hour, air them; then darken with a decoction of 1 lb. of logwood, 4 oz. of blue stone and 1 do. of copperas.

No. 54.---Snuff Brown.---To 5 lb.---Boil 2 lb. of fustick 12 oz. of cam wood, 4 do. of saunders for one hour, raise your colour with 4 do. of blue stone, enter your goods, boil for one hour, then air and darken off with copperas.

No. 55.---Another.---Make a weak decoction of black-oak bark and sumac, dissolve therein 5 oz. of blue stone, and run your goods therein for 15 minutes, then rinse, and boil off 2 lb, of fustick, 1 gal. of walnut hulls and 1-2 lb. cam wood for one hour, then enter your goods and boil for one hour more---air, and darken with copperas.

No. 56.---Brown.---Walnut hulls boiled will make a brown, and with any sort of red dye-stuff, alum and copperas or blue stone will make it of different shades.

No. 57.---Brown Olive---Dark.---To 5 lb.---Boil 3-4 lb. of fustick, 3-4 lb. of cam wood or saunders, 3-4 lb. of logwood for one hour, raise the colour with 4 oz. of alum, then enter your goods and boil for one hour---darken with copperas.

Another.---Boil 1 lb. of cam wood, saunders, or Brazil, 3-4 lb. fustick, 3-4 lb. logwood for one hour, then add 4 oz. of madder and 3 do. of alum, enter your goods, boil for one hour---darken with copperas.

Note.---The logwood boiled with other dye-stuffs, ought to be boiled in a bag and taken out before the goods are entered, otherwise it will make the goods spotted.

No. 58.---Olive.---To 5 lb.---Take 2 lb. of fustick and a little sumac, boil them for half an hour, then add the decoction to 5 oz. of logwood with 10 do. of alum and 4 do. of madder, boil your yarn for one hour---cool, and darken with 5 oz. of copperas.

No. 59.---Cinnamon.---To 5 lb.---Boil your yarn in a preparation of 10 oz. of alum and 4 do. of tartar for two hours, then rinse, and boil for one hour, add 1-2 lb. of saunders, 1-2 lb. of madder and 1 lb. of fustick, then boil your yarn therein for one hour---darken with copperas.

No. 60.---Another.---Boil for one hour 3-4 lb. bear wood, 1 1-2 lb. fustick, boil your yarn therein for one hour---darken with copperas.

No. 61.---Fawn Colour.---To 5 lb.---Take 4 oz. of saunders, 1 do. of fustick, 1-2 do. Brazil, and 1-2 do. of logwood, boil for one hour, then add 1-2 oz. of alum 1-2 do. of crude tartar, boil your yarn one hour and darken with 2 oz. of copperas.

No. 62.---Wine-Stone Colour.---To 5 lb.---Take 4 oz. of saunders and 4 do. of fustick, boil for half an hour; then boil your yarn therein for one hour, then darken with 4 oz. of blue stone. If you darken with copperas instead of blue stone it makes another shade.

No. 63.---Rich Red Drab.---To 5 lb.---Take 5 oz. of madder, 5 do. of fustick, and 1 gallon walnut hulls, boil them together for half an hour, then boil your yarn therein for one hour, and darken it off with 4,6, or 8 oz. of blue stone, according as you wish the shade.

No. 64.---Another Red Drab.---To 5 lb.---Take 5 oz. of madder, 4 do. of black-oak bark and 4 do. of sumac, boil half an hour, then add 1 oz. of alum, 1 do. of crude tartar, 2 do. solution of tin, No. 2, boil your yarn for one hour---darken with 4 oz. of copperas or 6 oz. of blue stone.

No. 65.---Drab in General.---Make a strong decoction of sumac and elder bark, run your goods through, one piece after the other, the first piece will be the darkest shade, the last the lightest; then darken with blue stone---it will produce a more bluish drab by darkening with copperas; other shades by adding logwood liquor; others by adding black-oak bark liquor, and still others by adding red-wood liquor. Where you can make a variety of shades, lime water or white chalk used with either, will produce other shades, or by mixing a little chemic, or by first making the goods a light pearl blue. Make the colours before fulling. Maple bark and sumac boiled for one hour, and then the yarn boiled for one hour more, then darkened with copperas, makes a fine blue drab or lead colour. Boil this lead colour in the liquor of walnut hulls, which makes a very good brown.

I will now describe the different shades of Green, and Natural Green, which is half blue and half yellow.

No. 66.---Green.---To 5 lb.---Colour your yarn first in the blue vat, No. 5 or 7, a light blue; wash it well, then take 1 1-4 lb. of alum and 5 oz. of crude tarter dissolved in water, and boil your goods therein for one hour, then rinse them well; then take 1-2 lb. of fustick, boil it for half an hour, take out the chips and raise the colour with 2 oz. of alum, then add to this yellow dye so much sulphate of indigo or chemic, No. 4, that you will perceive the liquor is a nice and handsome green; stir the dye well, then enter your pale blue goods and boil for two hours; after half an hour's boiling air your goods, when you will see whether you can get your wished-for colour. If it is too yellow add more chemic, then enter your goods and boil them, after which take them out and wash them clean.

You can make almost any shade, which it is not necessary to describe under different names. It is often unnecessarily done in dye-books. I will only add, if you want a grass or bluish green, add more chemic, and less chemic will make it more yellow. You can likewise colour different shades out of the same liquor, which varieties look so well in carpets. This colour is very permanent, owing to the blue it receives in the blue vat.

No. 67.---Bottle Green.---This is made exactly like No. 56, but after half an hour's boiling in the dye take it out and add logwood liquor and copperas, and boil your goods again. In this manner you can make as dark a shade as you like, even to an invisible green, which colour is shaded on black, with a green cast.

Another bottle green is made without the blue vat, but it is not so lasting, which is made in the following manner:

No. 68.---Boil 2 lb. of fustick for half an hour, then raise the colour with 4 oz. of alum, then add a decoction of 1 lb. of logwood. Boil your yarn for one hour, then darken it with copperas. You can make lighter shades by diminishing the dye-stuffs.

No. 69.---Saxon Green.---To 5 lb.---This is a fugacious colour like saxon blue, No. 8, and it will in no wise resist air or alkali, but is a very useful colour for carpeting, and is made thus:

Boil your yarn in a preparation of one lb. of alum and 4 oz. of crude tartar for two hours, rinse it; then fill your boiler with water and boil 2 lb. of fustick for half an hour, raise your liquor with 2 oz. of alum, then add as much chemic, No. 4, as you think may give you the shade required. You can likewise make a handsome bottle green out of this dye by darkening it with logwood liquor and copperas. You can make lighter shades by taking out the darkest and adding a little chemic and then boiling your yarn therein. In this manner you can have it as light as goslin green.

No. 70.---Invisible Green on Black Goods.---To. 5 lb.---If you have a blak (sic) piece of goods, and would wish to have another colour, then make a strong decoction of fustick or blackwood bark, raise the colour with 3-4 lb. of alum and 4 oz. of crude tartar, then add so much chemic that by stirring your dye it will look a bluish green---boil your goods therein for two hours, and you will have a beautiful colour.

No. 71.---Black.---To 5 lb.---I shall now give a few receipts for black---the first is made in Germany and Europe, in general on fine cloth. Dye your goods first a good pale blue in a blue vat, No. 5 or 7.

Prepare a strong decoction of sumac and elder, with 1-2 lb. of fustick, after boiling for one hour take out the dye-stuff and add 4 oz. of madder and 2 do. of crude tartar with 4 do. of blue-stone; then enter your goods and boil them for two hours, air and rinse them; then boil off 2 lb. of logwood for half an hour, run your goods for one hour; then cool, and dissolve 8 oz. of copperas, and 2 do. of verdigris; boil your goods again for one hour, then wash in soap suds. Sometimes the goods, after they are fulled, are again run through logwood liquor wherein copperas and verdigris have been dissolved.

No. 72.---Common Black.---To 5 lb.---Boil off 2 lb. of logwood, 8 oz. of fustick, sumac, and elder, for one hour, take out the dye-stuff, then enter your goods and boil them for two hours, take them out and air them; then add 8 oz. of copperas and of blue-stone, boil it again for one hour, and you will have a jet black.

No. 73.---Slate, Mouse, and Ash Colours.---These colours do not want a different description, as they are only lighter shades of black, and can all be made in the same liquor or dye.

Remark.---Wherever, in the foregoing receipts, fustick is mentioned, black-oak bark will do.

COTTON DYES

I will now describe the cotton dyes in all their various branches. As the Turkey red is very expensive, and in this country the dyeing comes as high as the cotton ready dyed, those that want to make use of it will do better to buy it; but I will give a substitute for it, which will be permanent enough for domestic use. I will here state that the cotton, before it is dyed, must be well boiled, on account of the vegetable glue that adheres to it, which must be removed that the dye may impregnate it. As there are several mordants to be used in dyeing cotton, I shall describe them as follows:

No. 74.---Lime-Water.---Get a well bound barrel, put in it a peck of unslacked lime, slack it and continue to put water in the barrel so long as there is a skim on the top; after stirring it up, if your lime water is good when you take any out fill it up again with water. Lime water, in dyeing browns and blacks, is a very good corrective and alternative when the goods do not get to the shades required, especially for cotton, but it will likewise do for silk.

No. 75.---Mordant to Cotton and Linen.---For yellow, green and red; dissolve 4 lb. of acetate of lead, (sugar of lead,) in two gallons of hot water in a half barrel, then dissolve 3 lb. of alum in six gal. of water, and add it to the sugar of lead solution, then stir it up and cover it over for use. When you use this liquor you must, after stirring it up, let it settle and use the clear liquor only. When weak, add more sugar of lead and alum.

No. 76.---Nitrate of Iron.---Get old iron, wash it clean so the rust is all off, then get 2 lb. of nitric acid, mix it with one quart of water, then take a woolen rag, dip into the aqua fortis liquor, rub it slightly over the iron, lay it in the sun to rust, then have a well bound barrel filled with water; when your iron is well rusted, wash it in the water in the barrel; rub the iron again with the acid, after rusting wash it in the barrel again as before, and so keep on till your water is well saturated with iron, then cover it well for use.

No. 77.---Acetate of Iron or Iron Liquor.---Get a well bound barrel, put therein about 50 lb. of old iron well cleaned from dirt, fill it with good vinegar, cover it up, and in three or four weeks it will be ready for use. But this liquor improves by age and the older it gets the better it is for use.

No. 78.---Muriate of Iron.---This is made the same way as No. 76, but instead of nitric acid take muriatic acid. (Sp't of salt.)

No. 79.---Bran Water.---Put wheat bran in a pine or cedar vessel, then scald it with boiling water. This is a necessary article in a dye house.

Indigo Blue.---For good standing blue on cotton, linen, and silk, see No. 6.

No. 80.---Logwood Blue.---To 5 lb.---Boil your cotton or linen in lie for one hour, wash it well; then boil off 6 oz. of logwood in 4 gallons of water for half an hour, take away the chips; then add 1-2 oz. of verdigris and 1 do. of alum, boil your cotton for 5 minutes and let it lay therein till cold, then wash it clean in water.

No. 81.---Prussian Blue.---To 5 lb.---Nitrate of iron solution, weakened with water, and your cotton steeped therein for 6 hours, will be a preparative for blue; then dissolve 1-4 lb. of Prussiate of potash in 1-2 gallon of water with 4 oz. of oil of vitriol; run your cotton through this till blue enough, then wring it well and wash it in a stream of water as soon as it comes out of the oxide of iron. The cotton must be well washed. You can dip one parcel after another in the nitrate of iron, and run it through the prussiate of potash till the colour is quite exhausted. The more the cotton is impregnated with the oxide of iron the darker will your colour be. This is a handsome colour but very fugacious; if the cotton after it is boiled, is first run in a solution of cloride of lime, it improves the colour very materially.

No. 82.---Sky Blue and Brown.---To 5 lb.---Give the goods as much colour as they will receive from blue vitriol dissolved in warm water, and then run it through lime-water; it will make a durable colour; run this blue through a solution of Prussiate of potash, and it will make a beautiful brown.

No. 83.--Red, Permanent Madder Dye.---To 5 lb., first operation.---Boil you (sic) cotton for one hour in soft water, then wash and dry it. Second operation; boil it in 2 lb. pearlash or lie, with 1 gallon of lime-water, No. 74, rinse and dry it. Third operation; boil it for two hours in water wherein 1 lb. of hard soap has been dissolved with 1-2 lb. of pearlash; wash it in hot water, then in cold water. Fourth operation; put in a vessel as much of the mordant, No. 75, as will cover the cotton; let it lay in soak for six hours, then wring it hard into the vessel and dry it before a warm stove. Fifth operation; put in a vessel, lime water, No. 74, as much as will be necessary to steep your cotton therein; squeeze it well with your hands through and through for ten minutes, then wring it hard and dry it; then twist it twice more through the same operation, that is in the fourth and fifth, strengthening the mordant and lime water every time with fresh lime and sugar of lead.

Note.---The mordant in the fourth and fifth operation must be heated hand hot. After you have it three times through fourth and fifth operation, go through the sixth also.

Take 1 lb. of pearlash, dissolve it in 1 quart of hot water, and melt therein 1-2 lb. of lard, then fill a bucket half full with hot water, put one-fifth part of the pearlash liquor to the water, then take 1 lb. of cotton, work it through and through with your hands, then wring it out; get more hot water to the same liquor, and another fifth part of the pearlash, and another pound of cotton, work it as before, and so go on till your cotton is through, then hang it up and dry it. Seventh operation; get about one peck of fresh sheep dung, put it in a tub, then put sufficient hot water thereon to cover your cotton, then work it after the sheep dung is well mixed with the water therein, and let it lay for 12 hours, every now and then turning and squeezing it, then wring and rinse it, wring it again and dry it. Eighth operation; prepare a strong sumac decoction, strain the liquor and work the cotton therein, and then let it lay for 12 hours; wring and dry it. Ninth operation; strengthen your mordant, or rather get a fresh supply of No. 65, heat it, and work and lay your cotton in for six hours, then wring and dry it. Tenth operation; fill your boiler with soft water, and as soon as hand hot put therein 3 lb. of good madder; then have your cotton, which has previously been wetted in hot water and well wrung, put on sticks over the kettle, let it then rest on the top and turn your cotton continually till your dye is boiling hot, which it should be in 15 minutes; then lay your cotton in the dye and keep it in a boiling heat for 30 minutes more, then take it out, wash, and dry it. Eleventh operation; fill your boiler with soft water, cut and dissolve 1 lb. of white soap, put it in your boiler when hot, then put in your dyed cotton and cover it well, that the steam cannot escape; then boil it a few minutes, let it stand till hand warm, then take it out, wash and dry it. If you want it more brilliant, lay your yarn in the mordant, No. 75, for 6 hours, rinse it; then boil off 4 lb. of Brazil wood for 2 hours, take out the chips, then raise the colour with 6 oz. of alum and 10 do. of muriate of tin, No. 3, stir it up and run your cotton through it for 10 or 15 minutes. This colour will stand washing but not bleaching, like Turkey red.

No. 84.---Brazil Red---Preparation.---Boil 1 lb. of cotton in water for one hour, then in lye for two hours, wring and wash it; then boil two hours in soap, and wash it first in warm, then in cold water, to get the soap out---3 oz. of hard soap is sufficient---then as much of the mordant liquor, No. 75, hand hot, as will steep it for six hours, then wring and dry it; then put in a bucket as much lime-water, No. 74, as will work your cotton conveniently, work it therein for 10 or 15 minutes, wring it dry. Heat your mordant liquor again and add fresh to it, No. 75, as may be necessary, steep it again for 6 hours, then dry it; then add more lime-water to the former, and work your cotton again for 15 minutes, repeat this for 3 times, then rinse lightly, when it is ready for colouring.

Take 1 lb. of Brazil wood, boil it for 2 hours, take out the chips, then add 2 oz. of alum, and 2 do. solution of tin, enter your wet cotton and boil it for half an hour, then let it lay therein till cold, wash and dry it. You can make this more permanent by putting 2 oz. of madder to the Brazil.

No. 85.---Dark Red.---Take the cotton prepared as in No. 84, steep it in a strong decoction of sumac, for 24 hours, rinse, and then colour it with Brazil, as in No. 84. You will improve it by steeping it once more in the mordant for six hours, after sumac steep, and before colouring.

No. 86.---Light Red, Inclining to Scarlet.---Prepare your cotton as in No. 84, then run it through a decoction of black-oak bark, then dye it in Brazil, as above.

No. 87.---Brown.---You can make all the different shades of brown with the above red colours, No. 84, 85, and 86. Put the iron liquor into a bucket and work your cotton therein for 15 minutes, then rinse and dry, or dissolve in hot water, 4 oz. of copperas to the pound; wash your cotton for 15 minutes.

No. 88.---Brown.---Work your cotton alternately, in a strong hot decoction of sumac and a solution of copperas in hot water, for four or five times, then run it through lime-water for 5 minutes, then run it through a strong decoction of quercitron bark, wash and dry it. You will get another shade by using the iron liquor, No. 77, state of copperas solution. Another shade by using the nitrate of iron.

No. 89.---Orange.---To 1 lb.---Make your water hot, and dissolve therein 1 oz. of aranetta, then add 2 oz. of alum and 2 do. pearlash, work your boiled cotton therein so hot that you can just bear your hand in it, for 15 minutes, then wash and dry it in the shade.

No. 90.---Buff.---Take 1 lb. of copperas, dissolve it in hot water in one vessel, and strong lime-water, or lie (sic) or a solution of pot or pearlash, in another vessel; then work your cotton therein alternately for one, two, three, or four times, as you would wish to have the shade, which will make it a deep green colour; but let it hang in the air and it will change to a buff, more or less dark according to the dipping. To make the orange, No. 89, more permanent, it is first dyed buff, wash it first in clean water in either case, then take hot water, with 1-2 pint of soft soap and 4 oz. of lard, dissolve them in hot lye, put them together and work your cotton therein, as it will be the means of softening the cotton, then rinse and dry it.

No. 91.---Permanent Green.---Make your cotton a light blue in the cold blue vat, No. 6, rinse, and then work it in the mordant liquor and lime-water as in No. 84, then dye it in yellow dye, No. 92.

No. 92.---Permanent Yellow.---Prepare your cotton with Brazil wood, as in No. 84, then prepare a strong decoction of quercitron bark, raise it by scraping therein a little chalk, when hand hot work your cotton therein for 15 minutes, wash and dry it; then prepare a strong decoction of quercitron bark, raise it with 1 oz. of blue stone, wash your cotton for 10 minutes and let it dry till cold, and you will have a fine good colour for any use, and of different shades, if you regulate the shades in the blue vat, by colouring some brighter and some darker. By adding logwood liquor to the yellow dye, you can make different shades of dark green.

No. 93.---Another Green.---Dye your cotton a pale blue, as in No. 6, rinse it; then lay it in a hot solution of 3 oz. of alum and 2 do. of blue stone for 12 hours, then dye it with the quercitron bark, as in No. 6.

No. 94.---Another Dark Green is Made..---Steep your cotton in a hot solution of 4 oz. of alum, for 24 hours; then make a decoction of 4 oz. of logwood; raise with 1 do. of pearlash; another decoction of black oak bark, raised with 2 oz. of blue-stone, work your cotton hand hot in those two decoction alternately for 3 or 4 times, then put the two liquors together, lay your cotton in till cold, wash it, and if necessary saden it with copperas.

No. 95.---Drabs.---Combine your cotton with oxide of iron, that is, steep it for 4 hours either in a solution of copperas or iron liquor No. 77, or nitrate of iron No. 76, then have a weak decoction of black-oak bark, raised with a little chalk, run your cotton through hot---you can make different shades according to the strength of the oxide of iron previously used.

No. 96.---Olive.---By raising the bark solution with 2 oz. of blue-stone or chalk, as in No. 96, you will have a good olive, which can be darkened by adding logwood or sumac liquor.

No. 97.---Purple.---Dye your cotton middle blue in vat No. 6; prepare it red, as in No. 84, with a mordant, then dye it with Brazil as in No. 84---lighter shades are made by decreasing the colour which will make a violet with iron liquor, as in No. 77; chocolate colour of different shades, according to the strength of the dye.

No. 98.---Common Purple.---Boil 1-2 lb. of logwood for half an hour, take out the chips, then dissolve therein 2 oz. of alum, boil your cotton for half an hour; then let it lay in till cold, rinse, and dry it in the shade; lighter colours can be made in the same liquor by adding more alum, it will make a peach blossom.

Now I will describe the colours with solution of tin as a mordant.

No. 99.---Quercitron Bark.---Boil your cotton and dye it with Quercitron bark, as in No. 24.

No. 100.---Red.---Boil your cotton in sumac liquor, wring it well; then lay it in a strong decoction of sumac for 24 hours, wring it hard, then boil one pound of nigra aqua to every lb. of cotton, for 2 hours, in double the quantity of water that will be sufficient for 1 lb. to colour, then have 2 vessels, fill one with as much boiling water as it necessary to dip your cotton in, and put half of your red boiling liquor in your other vessel; then put 3 oz. of solution of tin, in your hot water as in No. 2, for every lb. of cotton, hang it on a stick and turn it in this liquor for 8 or 10 minutes, take it out and drain it---then put it into your red liquor, turn it for 15 minutes, wring it slightly, throw away that liquor, take the balance of your red dye, enter your cotton and turn it for 15 minutes more, rinse it, and you will have a very fine colour.

No. 101.---Scarlet.---Boil your cotton in water, and lay it in a strong decoction of sumac for 24 hours; wring and colour it exactly as in No. 100: instead of hot water prepare a weak decoction of black oak bark, put therein your solution of tin, and then run it through the Nicaragua liquor as above.

No. 102.---Spanish brown.---Dye it the same as in No. 100; then turn it for 15 minutes in the iron liquor, as in No. 77.

Note.---After having used the iron liquor, in any colour, you must always put it back again into the barrel to the iron; occasionally, fill it up with fresh vinegar.

No. 103.---Black.---Boil your cotton in sumac liquor, then lay it in a strong decoction of sumac for 24 hours, wring it well, then put as much of the iron liquor, No. 77, into a vessel as is necessary to wash your goods, then put lime-water into another vessel, then work your goods alternately back and forh (sic) till all looks pretty black; if it should not get black enough, dissolve 4 oz. of copperas in sumac liquor, run it 2 or 3 times more---every time wring it hard, and let it have the atmospheric air at intervals of a few minutes, then when it comes out of the lime-water last, rinse it; thus working the goods back and forth can be done, with the liquor hand warm; then make a decoction of logwood, throw it boiling over your goods, and let it lay till cold; wring it hard; wash it clean. If your cotton should have a rusty cast run it again through weak lime-water.

No. 104.---Slate.---This colour is only a lighter shade than black, can be made in the same or in fresh liquor, but in a weaker state.

Mouse and Ash Colours.---Mouse and ash colours are also only light shades of black.

SILK AND ITS COLOURS.

I shall now give a description of silk and its colours. Silk is an animal production, and has great cohesion with the animal gum, and cannot receive the colour until this gum is loosened and extracted. Silk has also, naturally a glossy appearance, which the dyer must always try to preserve, as artificial gloss will only last for a while, which the dyer of course must put on such silks as have been in use, as in garments &c.

I will here describe a mordant, which is always used either hand warm or cold, as boiling heat would destroy the glossy appearance.

No. 105.---Mordants for Silk.---Dissolve 2 lb. alum and 2 oz. cream of tartar in 4 gallons hot water, and preserve it for use. You must always keep this solution in this strength by adding more alum, as soon as it gets exhausted. Silk has commonly a yellowish colour which the gum increases, and must therefore be extracted, and the silk made as white and clear as possible, to receive the light colours, which is done as follows:

Take clear soft water, dissolve therein to every pound of silk 1-4 lb. of white soap, (have your boiler well scoured,) then put your silk neatly together in 4 ounce hanks, tied very loosely with fine cotton or linen strings, six or eight times round, then put it into a fine, thin cotton or gauze bag; enter it in the boiler and boil it 2 hours, with care that the bag is always covered with the liquor and not pressed together. After boiling 2 hours take it out, drain it, and after cooling so that you can work it with your hands, wring it well, then wash it in clean strained hot bran water, after, in clear soft warm water, and then in cold. If you want it whiter, put in oil of vitriol, cork, flour, rosin or sugar, till quite black, then ascidulate water therewith, so that the ascid (sic) can be tasted, lay in the silk for 6 hours, then wring it well, wash it clean in running water, and dry it. If you want to preserve it in a white state, blue it, by dissolving 1-4 oz. of Prusian (sic) blue in 6 gallons of water, lay the silk therein for 2 hours, if it should feel rough, run it through warm water wherein a little soap has been dissolved. Indigo will do as well for bluing as the Prussian blue. Sulphuring silk can be done for white, as will be described hereafter.

No. 106.---Indigo blue.---Wet your silk, and in any shade, dye it in the vat either No. 5 or 6, then rinse it well, and dissolve 1 oz. of white soap to the silk per lb. in 2 gallons of soft water, add 1 pint of lime-water thereto and wash the silk therein, afterwards in warm bran water, then wash it in clear water. It is more convenient to prepare a lather with lime-water and white soap; when silk wants washing, use of that lather and warm water, and wring your goods; it preserves the soft and glossy appearance of them; dissolve 1-4 lb. of white soap in 1-2 gallon of hot lime-water.

No. 107.---Turkish blue.---To 1 lb. silk.---Put 1-2 oz. of fine powdered cochineal into a well scoured boiler of boiling water, boil it for a few minutes, then add 2 oz. of alum and 2 oz. of murio sulphate of tin No. 2, boil for 30 minutes, then take it out and wash it well, fill your boiler again with fresh water and when hot put therein as much chemic No. 4, as will make the liquor appear a dark blue, raise the dye with 2 oz. of alum, enter the silk, and boil it for 30 minutes, then wash it clean in bran water, then rinse it in fresh water. Lighter shades can be made, after the first lb. is dyed in the cochineal liquor; add 1 oz. more of alum and 1 1-2 do. solution of tin; boil another lb. of silk therein for 30 minutes, take it out and rinse it, and then add 1 oz. more of alum with a little chemic, then boil the second parcel of silk therein. Note.---Silk should never boil hard; the water should be kept in a gentle heated agitation.

No. 108.---Saxon blue.---Wet your silk in warm water, then lay it in the mordant No. 105, for 48 hours, then take it out and rinse it well, have your boiler filled with clear water; when not put therein as much of the chemic as you wish to have in the dye; then add 1 oz. solution of tin No. 2, enter your silk and simmer it for 30 minutes, then rinse in warm water mixed with 1 pint of the lather, then wash it in clean water.

No. 109.---Pearl blue.---Add to the exhausted dye No. 108, 2 oz. alum and a decoction of 1-2 do. Brazil, run the silk through it for 5 or 10 minutes, then wash it with water and lather.

No. 110.---Ultra Marine.---Take 2 lb. or any quantity of muriatic acid, dissolve therein as much copper filings as it will dissolve, then put the clear liquor into another vessel, and add sp't of ammoniac to it by degrees till it is saturated, then have fresh warm water and add as much of the solution as will make the liquid a fine pale blue, and the liquor taste considerably sour, then run the silk for 15 minutes.

No. 111.---Sky blue.---Give the silk as much as it will take in, of a solution of bluestone, then run it through lime-water, which makes it very durable; then wash it in bran water.

No. 112.---Prussian blue.---Dissolve 5 oz. of copperas, run your silk therein for 10 minutes, rinse it clean, then have a solution of Prussiate of potash in another vessel, add a little sulphuric acid and immerse the silk in it for ten minutes, rinse it; then get 1 pint chamber lie (sic), boil and skim it, then put it in about 4 gal. of water, add 1 gill of vinegar, and run your silk through, then wash in clean water.

No. 113.--Prussian blue of different shades.---Impregnate each parcel of silk with a different quantity of the oxide of iron by immersing it in a solution of different strength for the deeper shades.

Take the iron liquor, No. 77, and for the lighter the sulphate of iron, immerse in each solution 2 parcels, then rinse it in separate waters; each parcel is then dipped in distinct baths of the prussiate of potash, the quantity corresponding with the oxide of iron previously united to it, (that is, the silk that had the strongest solution of iron must likewise have the strongest prussiate of potash solution.) With this precaution the desired shades will be obtained.

The lighter shade will have a greenish cast, but washing well in running water will produce the colour to a certainty.

No. 114.---Dark Red.---For 1 lb., prepare a decoction of 4 oz. of nut-galls, by pounding them fine and boilinn (sic) them in 2 gal. of water for 30 minuets (sic), strain the liquor, then immerse the silk therein for 24 hours, wring it well into the liquor; (this gall liquor you can always use, by adding fresh galls boiled in water,) then dissolve 4 oz. of alum, 1 do. sal ammoniac, and 1 do. cream of tartar, dissolve these drugs in boiling water and steep your silk therein for 48 hours; then boil off 1 lb. of Brazil for 2 hours, strain the liquor, and then add 2 oz. of madder, enter your silk that had previously been rinsed after it came out of the alum liquor, and keep it in boiling heat or very slow boiling for 30 minutes, let it cool off for 30 minutes, then wring it well and wash it with water and lather, then rinse it in clean water.

No. 115.---Red-brown.---Dissolve 4 oz. of copperas and 1 oz. of blue stone in warm water, run your silk in dye No. 114, till it is brown enough, or get iron liquor, No. 77, and work your silk therein, which will give a brown of a different shade.

No. 116.---Light Red.---Gall the silk with 2 oz. of nut-gall for 24 hours, wring it; then make a mordant of 4 oz. of alum and 2 oz. cream of tartar, dissolve them in hot water, then steep the silk therein for 48 hours, then wring and rinse it. Boil off 1 lb. of Brazil for 2 hours, settle it with cold water, and decant the clear liquor, then add 2 oz. solution of tin, No. 1, stir it up and enter the silk, simmer it for 45 minutes, let it lay till half cold, then air it and wash it in warm water with lather, then in bran-water, and then in a running stream, as usual.

No. 117.---Blood Red.---Gall the silk in 4 oz. of nut-gall, for 24 hours, then steep it in alum mordant, No. 105, for 48 hours, then get 1-4 oz. of aranetta dissolved in hot water, add 4 oz. of pearlash and 1-2 oz. sal ammoniac previously rinsed, work the silk therein for 30 minutes, rinse it again; then prepare a decoction of 1 lb. Brazil, by boiling it 2 hours, decant from the dye-stuff, raise the liquor with 1 oz. of alum, simmer the silk for 45 minutes, then wash it as usual.

No. 118.---Scarlet.---Steep the silk in No. 105, for 48 hours, rinse it, then dissolve 1 oz. aranetta in hot water, add 1-2 oz. pearlash, turn the silk for 30 minutes, rinse it, then boil 1-2 lb. Brazil for 2 hours, decant the liquor; then add 2 oz. solution of tin No. 3, and simmer the silk for 1 hour, wash it in clean bran water, and then in running water.

No. 119.---Crimson.---Make a light shade of blue in the vat No. 6, then dye it in No. 117.

No. 120.---Lighter Crimson.---Make a light shade of blue in the vat No. 6, then dye it in No. 119.

No. 121.---Crimson of another kind.---Steep your silk in solution of 4 oz. of alum, 2 do. nut-gall, 2 do. sal ammoniac, and 2 do. pearlash, dissolve these articles in boiling water, enter the silk and simmer it for a few minutes, then let it lay in it for 24 hours, rinse it, and then boil off 1 lb. of Brazil for 2 hours, decant it off, then raise the colour with 2 oz. of alum and 2 do. of pearlash, enter the silk, simmer it for 1 hour, then put out the fire, and let it lay 30 minutes longer in the dye, then rinse it in clear water, then run it through lime-water; then wash it with a strong white soap lather, then rinse it in bran and in clear water, as usual.

No. 122.---Pinks.---These are made the same as crimson, No. 121, only the proportions of dye-stuffs very much decreased to the shade required.

No. 123.---Scarlet, with Cochineal.---See woolen dye, No. 14; but instead of boiling fast, only simmer it.

No. 124.---Pink of different shades.---Steep your silk in mordant, No. 105, for 24 hours, rinse; then take 1-2 oz. of powdered cochineal, boil it for a few minutes, then add 2 oz. solution of tin, No. 3, enter your silk and simmer for half an hour, then run it through lime-water, wash in lather and bran-water, and then running water, with Brazil liquor; this way you can make all the variety of shades.

No. 125.---Darkened with Madder.---Steep your silk in mordant, No. 105, rinse; then put 1-2 lb. of madder in your boiler with water, when hand hot add 2 oz. solution of tin, No. 1; then enter your silk in a gauze bag (that the madder grains cannot enter) very loosely, simmer your silk, or rather keep it in a boiling heat for one hour, then wash it as usual. This is a very permanent colour, and will make a very permanent dye.

No. 126.---Brown.---By running it through the acetate of Iron, No. 77.

No. 127.---Browns in General.---Steep your silk in 1-4 lb. of nut-galls, then in mordant, No. 105, for 48 hours; then make a decoction of 1-4 lb. of Brazil, 1-4 lb. sanders, 2 lb. madder, and 4 oz. of fustic; boil it for two hours, decant off, then simmer your silk for one hour, darken it with copperas, blue-stone, or iron-liquor, No. 77; wash it with lather, bran, and clear water. With all the different varieties with lather, bran, and clear water. With all the different varieties of red, dye-wood mixed with fustic, quercitron-bark or aranetta, you can make all the different shades of brown, the mordant is the same as in No. 127, the darkening likewise, and the washing also; brown inclining to yellow, take according to proportion, more yellow dye and less red, a lively colour is given in.

No. 128.---Brown.---Run your sky-blue, No. 111, in a solution of prussiate of potash, run your silk through the lime-water, then wash it as usual.

No. 129.---Purple.---Dye it middle blue in blue vat, No. 6, wash it in water, then steep it in mordant, No. 105, rinse it; then boil off 1-4 lb. Brazil with 2 oz. logwood, boil for an hour, decant your liquor; then add 1 oz. solution of tin, No. 3, and 2 oz. pearlash, then enter your silk and simmer it for one hour, run it through lime-water, then wash as usual.

No. 130.---Another.---Steep your silk in mordant, No. 105, for 24 hours, rinse, and boil off 1 lb. of logwood, and 1-4 lb. Brazil; decant your liquor, raise the colour with 1 oz. of alum, and 2 of tin liquor, No. 3, simmer your silk for one hour, run it through lime-water and wash as usual.

No. 131.---Lilach.---This is a lighter shade of purple, No. 129, and 130. Different shades can be made by diminishing the dye-stuffs.

No. 132.---Cinnamon Colours.---Steep in mordant, No. 105, for 24 hours, then wash; then boil 1 oz. sanders, 1 oz. madder, and 4 oz. fustic for one hour, decant your dye, and add 1 pint of iron-liquor, No. 77, simmer your silk for one hour---wash as usual.

No. 133.---Another.---Run your silk through warm water with a little lime-water, then boil for one hour, darken it with copperas.

All the cinnamon colours can be made in different shades by diminishing the dye-stuffs, and then darkening. The proportion is commonly one part of red and two parts of yellow---with a slight mordant the colours become bright.

No. 134.---Fawn.---This colour is a very light cinnamon with a little more darkening in it.

No. 135.---Buff.---This is a still lighter shade of cinnamon and fawn colours; made in the same manner; but they are all run through the lime-water and then washed as usual after dyeing.

No. 136.---Orange.---Dissolve in hot water 1 1-2 oz. aranetta; then add 2 oz. of soda or 2 oz. of pearlash, with 2 oz. of alum; work your wet silk therein for one hour, run it through lime-water, then wash it.

No. 137.---Yellow of different shades.---Make a decoction of black-oak bark, then put therein 1 oz. of alum and 3 oz. solution of tin, No. 3, enter your wet silk and work it for fifteen minutes, take it out, wring and wash it; then add to the same liquor 2 oz. more tin liquor, run another shade; add 1 oz. more tin liquor, run another shade; add 1-2 oz. more, and run another shade if you want it a greenish cast. Add every time to the tin liquor 2 oz. cream of tartar---this makes the most brilliant shades imaginable; and the varieties are from a bright orange to a straw colour, with the iron-liquor, No. 77, put first as a basis; as iron-liquor and nut-galls, or both, make different shades of light brown and buff colours.

No. 138.---Green.---Colour your silk in blue vat No. 6 of different shades, rinse; then steep it in the mordant for 48 hours, rinse again, then make a strong decoction of fustic or black-oak bark, or both mixed, decant the dye, then add 2 oz. of bluestone, to raise the colour, run your silk through it, first the darkest shade of blue, then the next, every time adding a little bluestone, then add to your dye a little chemic and 1 oz. solution of tin, No. 3; run your silk as before, adding every time a little chemic, then you will have a good, permanent colour,---wash as usual.

No. 139.---Bottle-Green.---Steep your silk for 24 hours in No. 105, rinse; then boil off 1 lb. of fustic, raised with 1-2 lb. of blue-stone---have in another vessel boiling-hot water, put therein as much chemic as will make your liquor a handsome marine blue to the eye---raise it with a little chalk---then immerse your silk in the blue dye for five minutes; wring it, and enter it in the yellow dye for five minutes, wring it again, and put it in the blue dye, and again in the yellow till you have the wished-for colour.

N.B.---If you want a blue-green, take more chemic, and if yellow, less chemic, and you can make a different shade.

No. 140.---Bottle-Green.---Run your silk in blue vat, No. 6, rinse; then make a strong decoction of fustic, raise it with 2 oz. of alum and 1 oz. of blue vitriol, then add the decoction of 4 oz. of logwood, simmer your silk therein for 1 hour, wring it---then add 1 quart of iron-liquor, No. 77, handle your silk 15 minutes more; if necessary, darken it with copperas,---wash as usual.

No. 141.---Another.---Make a strong decoction of fustic, raise it with 2 oz. of alum, 1 oz. of bluestone, then add chemic to make it a handsome light green, run your silk for fifteen minutes, then add 2 oz. of madder, and the decoction of 4 oz. of logwood, simmer your silk for 1 hour, then darken it off with iron-liquor and copperas,---wash it as usual.

No. 142.---Olive.---Olive is a lighter colour of bottle-green, the yellow predominates, and so you can make any shade you please.

No. 143.---Black.---As black is a colour very much used in silk, and is a very fashionable one in almost every season, but when rusty it is abominable. I will therefore give a colour which will defy any rust: Dye your silk a pale blue in blue vat, No. 6, rinse; then make a vat with urine,---put 5 lb. of copperas into a half barrel, then put urine into an iron pot or boiler, simmer it for one hour, skim off the scum which rises, then let it get cold and settle; then take the chamber-lie (sic) and pour it in the tub over the copperas which it will dissolve; this liquor when weakened must always be strengthened by adding urine prepared as above, with copperas; this liquor is called urine sulphate of iron. After your silk is made blue, as above, then steep it in a decoction of 4 oz. of nut-galls for 48 hours---wring it well, and give it a good airing; then have another half barrel nearly filled with the iron liquor, No. 77; then take your silk and work it in the iron liquor for ten minutes, (cold or hand-warm,) wring and air it; then work the silk for ten minutes in the urine sulphate of iron, wring and air it, and so work it for five or six times alternately; then take 4 oz. of cloride of lime dissolved in sufficient water, stir it well, let it settle; then take the clear liquor and run your silk therein for fifteen minutes, then run it again in the urine and iron liquor, and again in the cloride of lime, then you will have a good black; but if it feels rather rough boil 4 oz. of logwood in a sufficient quantity of water for one hour, put your silk in the decanted liquor and let it stand till cold, then run it through weak lime-water, then strong lather, bran, and clear water, and you will have a black never to be altered.

N.B..---If you have no cloride of lime convenient, lime-water will answer as a substitute.

No. 144.---Another.---Steep your silk in a decoction of 4 oz. nut-gall, then make a decoction of 1-4 lb. of fustic and 1-4 lb. of logwood, decant your liquor after boiling one hour, then add 1 oz. cream of tartar, 2 oz. of madder scalded, and the clear liquor taken, enter your silk and simmer for half an hour, wring and air; then run it through lime-water, then run it again for ten minutes in the former liquor, in which 4 oz. of copperas had been dissolved, run it again in the lime-water, repeating three or four times, then pour over it a decoction of logwood of 4 oz.---wash as before.

No. 145.---Slate-Colours.---These are the lighter shades of black, and can be made after the black dyes, No. 143 and 144.

No. 146.--Drab and Dove.---These are all made with quercitron bark in a very weak state---raised either with copperas or bluestone, and then run through a diluted iron liquor; if a reddish cast is wanting, take a little madder liquor or red dye, of any kind.

No. 147.---Silver-Gray.---This is the lightest shade of grays, and can be made with a very weak decoction of nut-galls and a weak solution of copperas or iron liquor.

TO DYE FEATHERS AND BRISTLES.

I will here give a few receipts to dye feathers and bristles.

No. 148.---Green.---Soak your stuff in warm water, then dissolve and mix 1 oz. of verdigris and 1 oz. of verditter, in a quart of weak gum-water---dye it hand-warm.

No. 149.---Red.---Boil 1 oz. of Brazil in 1 quart of vinegar, decant it; then add 1-4 oz. of vermillion and 1-2 oz. of alum with a little gum arabic---soak your stuff first in warm water, then dye it warm.

No. 150.---Blue.---Have boiling water, add chemic, as you wish to have your shade---dissolve a little gum, add it with 1 oz. of alum---soak your feathers or bristles first in hot water then dye hot.

Note.---I will only add in closing this little work, that where nut-galls are used a strong sumac decoction is nearly as good.

APPENDIX

TO DISCHARGE COLOURS

As there are colours sometimes too dark, or that a different colour is desired, I will say a few words on discharging colours that contain oxide of iron, such as browns, dark or bottle-greens, purple, lilach, drabs, greys, and blacks. Heat water in a boiler, put therein so much oil of vitriol as to make it as sour as diluted vinegar, so that it tastes considerably acid--stir your liquor well and run your goods as quick as possible, till all the oxide of iron is discharged; wash it well in fresh water so that by sucking the stuff you cannot taste the acid any more; then proceed to colouring whatever colour you please. Indigo blue cannot be discharged, because it is a substantial colour, as no colour in which mineral or vegetable acids are used can be discharged with sulphuric acid; but those dyed with acid, such as chemic blue and green, can be discharged with alkali, potash, pearlash, or lye. Silk frocks, shawls, or other garments, can be likewise discharged in the same manner. After washing in clear water, wash it again with the lather, that is, lime-water and soap; then dye in the respective dyes described before. Silk garments, after being coloured, must be stiffened with gum arabic, and dried and ironed on the wrong side.

Ribins.---Ribins are dyed of any colour as in silk dyes described: after washing them well, have your gum-water in a bowl and rub it with a sponge on the wrong side with the gum-water; iron before it gets quite dry; any colour of silk that should be black, needs no discharge, but well cleansed with soap, and then dyed in either dye No. 143 or 144, well washing in lather, bran-water, &c., and then dried; then take sweet oil or melted lard, put very little of this grease on a soft brush,---a hair brush is best---and brush your silk occasionally---supplying the brush with grease; then wash it well in soap made in a lather with lime-water; stiffen it with gum-water iron it when damp on the wrong side.

N.B.---Garments or wove silk must not be wrung, but only drained.

Bonnets, Leghorn or Straw, dyed Black.---Soak your bonnet in lime-water for 24 hours, or if you have the copperas solution in urine it is better---take it out and air it; then make a strong decoction of logwood, add 2 oz. of copperas, then put your bonnet in a bucket and pour your logwood liquor therein and let it stand till cold; then press it over a block; after it is quite dry rub it over with a grease brush, slightly greased; then dissolve glue, rub it over with a sponge, press the bonnet again, at the same time when stiff enough, give it one coat of black varnish, press it again, then give it another coat, which finishes it.

Veils.---Are dyed black as in No. 143 or 144; then wash them clean, stiffen with gum-water and clap it in your hands, then pin it on a piece of cloth to dry.

APPENDIX.

Green Veils.---Take 2 oz. of alum, dissolve it in hot water, steep your veil for 24 hours, rinse it; then fill two pans with boiling water, put in one pan as much chemic, No. 4, to make your water middle blue, put in the other pan 2 oz. tumeric---work your veil alternately in the blue, then yellow, till your colour is a pretty green; wash it and stiffen with gum-water, then pin it out to dry.

To Scour Cloth Coats and Pantaloons.---Beat and brush out the dirt well out of the cloth to be scoured, which will show you every spot; wet the spots with spirit of wine and then rub casteel soap thereon, and let it stand for 1 hour, then wash it off with a brush and bran-water, brush it downward with the nap. To paint-spots take spirits of turpentine, and if necessary whip the dust out and scour the whole garment as before; then rub the soiled places with soap---then take boiling bran-water, add thereto 4 oz. of pearlash, 1 beef's gall, if convenient, if not, 1 pint of chamber-lye, brush your garment with a stiff brush with the nap. After brushing it so that all the spots are out take clean water and wash it down well with the brush, then with fresh water; then take to a coat, 1-2 pint of flaxseed, boil it in a quart of water, then strain the seeds from the liquor, and brush your scoured cloth with a hard brush, which will give the cloth a fine gloss as good as new. If the garment is faded you can renew the colour by putting into the flaxseed when boiling, 1-4 lb. copperas. Brush your coat or pants with the nap, then let it get perfectly dry, then press it, with a wet cloth between the iron. Flaxseed boiled with a little isinglass, put on with a brush on cloth or cassinet when the nap is raised in fulling mills, makes the goods far more brilliant.

Green Spots taken out of Linen, Cotton, and Silk.---Take magnesia in the lump, wet it in soft water and rub the spots well with it; in half an hour's time brush it off, and the spots will disappear, if not entirely the first, surely and certainly on the second application.

To Scour Raw Wool.---To 12 gallons of water take 3 gallons of urine prepared by boiling it together for a few minutes---when hand hot enter your wool and soak it. When the grease is loose, wash in clear water; as your urine gets weaker, and you have not enough, dissolve every time before you enter another parcel, 1-2 pint of salt in it---with the addition of salt you can scour as much as you please; with one bucket full of urine and 1 gallon of fish salt you can scour from five to six hundred pounds.

Bleaching.---Woolen yarn after it is washed clean with soap, and rinsed; prepare a barrel, hogshead, or any other vessel that you can shut up closely, put sticks inside crosswise, put brimstone in the bottom in an iron or earthen vessel with burning coals, then put your wet, but drained yarn on the sticks, cover it well so that no brimstone gas can escape, and in 12 or 24 hours your wool will be as white as possible, unless you had not a sufficiency---in this case add more; afterwards rinse and blue it with indigo.

APPENDIX.

Bleaching Cotton in 48 hours as White as Snow.---To 10 lb. of yarn, take 1 1-2 lb. unslacked lime, dissolve it in sufficient water, then take the milky lye, boil your cotton for five hours therein, wring and wash it clean; then dissolve 1 lb. cloride of lime in sufficient water, decant in a pine or cedar tub, and lay your cotton therein for 12 hours, then drain, and lay it in sour water, (water asidulated with oil of vitriol,) so that you can taste the water sour, wash it again, then boil it for 3 hours in water wherein 1-2 lb. pearlash has been dissolved, wash it again, put fresh water over the sediment of cloride of lime, stir it up and put the clear liquor into the former, then lay your cotton in it for 12 hours, drain and wash it; lay it again in sour water for 4 hours, then wash it well and blue it with indigo.

Chemical Essence of Soap to take out Stains and Grease on Wool, Silk, Cotton, and Linen.---Take 1 quart of water, 1 oz. pearlash, 2 oz. white vegetable soap, boil these three ingredients into a thin paste; then add 1 quart spirit of wine, 1 pint of water of ammonia; let it stand five days and it will be fit for use.

Shake the essence well, and wet the spot therewith, let it dry, then wash it off; if the first wetting does not remove it, a second surely will, and leave a fine gloss; but if tea-stains or iron-moulds, which are not so easily taken out, will still show themselves, the following receipt will surely be beneficial:

When lovely Woman tilts her saucer,
And finds too late that tea will stain---
What ever made a lady *crosser*?---
What art can wash all white again?
The only art the stain to cover,---
To hide the spot from every eye;
And wear an unsoiled dress above her---
The proper colour is to **DYE**.

TO MAKE BLACK INK.

I will conclude by offering a receipt for excellent black ink.---Boil 6 oz. logwood in 3 pints of water for half an hour, so that you will have a quart of liquor, decant off and add 2 oz. of powdered nut-galls, 1 oz. of clean copperas, 1-2 oz. of gum arabic powdered, and a few cloves, which keep the ink from moulding. Let it stand for two weeks in a warm place, then it will be fit for use.

TABLE OF CONTENTS.

TABLE OF CONTENTS.

MORDANTS.